SCARY PLACES

Mummy Lairs

by Michael Burgan

Consultant: Paul F. Johnston, PhD
Washington, D.C.

BEARPOR
PUBLISHII

New York, New York

Credits

Cover and Title Page, © LANBO/Shutterstock, Aleksandar Mijatovic/Shutterstock, and MAEADV/Shutterstock; 4-5, © Kim Jones; 6, © Danita Delimont Stock Photography/Newscom; 7L, © Eye Ubiquitous/SuperStock; 7R, © Ivan Alvarado/Reuters/Landov; 8, © The Print Collector/Alamy; 9, © Kenneth Garrett/National Geographic/Getty Images; 10, © AP Photo/Alessandro Fucarini; 11, © Tony Gentile/Reuters/Newscom; 12, © Oklahoma HIstorical Society; 13, © University of Oklahoma, Western History Collection, Rose #3065; 14, © Alain Nogues/Sygma/Corbis; 15T, © Science Faction/SuperStock; 15B, © Vladimir Mashatin/EPA/Newscom; 16, © Vienna Report Agency/Sygma/Corbis; 17, © AP Photo/Winfried Rothermel; 18, © Lars Horn/Baghuset; 19T, © Carlos Muñoz-Yagüe/Photo Researchers Inc.; 19B, © Robert Harding Picture Library/SuperStock; 20, © Roger Ressmeyer/Corbis; 21L, © Photos 12/Alamy; 21R, © Jonathan S. Blair/National Geographic/Getty Images; 22, © Douglas Peebles Photography/Alamy; 23, © Will & Deni McIntyre/Photo Researchers/Getty Images; 24, © Richard Weil; 25, © AP Photo; 26, © Cubo Images/SuperStock; 27L, © Thierry Berrod/Mona Lisa Production/Photo Researchers, Inc.; 27R, © Photosani/Shutterstock; 31, © Jose Ignacio Soto/Shutterstock.

Publisher: Kenn Goin
Editorial Director: Adam Siegel
Creative Director: Spencer Brinker
Design: Dawn Beard Creative
Cover Design: Dawn Beard Creative and Kim Jones
Photo Researcher: Picture Perfect Professionals, LLC

Library of Congress Cataloging-in-Publication Data

Burgan, Michael.
  Mummy lairs / by Michael Burgan.
      p. cm. — (Scary places)
  Includes bibliographical references and index.
  ISBN 978-1-61772-568-5 (library binding) — ISBN 1-61772-568-4 (library binding)
  1. Mummies—Juvenile literature. I. Title.
  GN293.B87 2013
  393'.3—dc23

                                    2012018189

ublishing Company, Inc., 45 West 21st Street, Suite 3B,
e United States of America.

Contents

Imagine finding the body of a person who has been dead for hundreds or even thousands of years. Yet instead of seeing a **corpse** that has rotted away, you see a body that looks almost as if it could still be alive. How is that possible? The dead person was turned into a mummy!

Some mummies have been found hidden in **tombs**. These tombs are sometimes called lairs—secret hiding places that may be filled with treasures and, according to some, **curses** as well. Other mummies have been found outdoors. Usually the bodies were buried in dry, rocky ground, but sometimes they were trapped in ice or stuck in the ancient mud of a swamp.

How and why are people—and even some animals—made into mummies? You'll find out as you explore 11 true tales of mummies from around the world. Among them are 7,000-year-old mummies who were welcomed into people's homes, a 3,000-year-old mummy who is said to have put a curse on those who unearthed it, and a modern mummy whom people line up to see—while they still have the chance.

The Oldest Mummies

El Morro, Chile

In 1983, workers near El Morro, Chile, were using a machine with a sharp metal blade to dig a hole for a water pipe. The workers knew they would uncover a lot of rocks and dirt as they got the job done. What they didn't expect was that they would also dig up a burial ground full of ancient American mummies. In fact, the site turned out to be the resting place of the oldest mummies ever discovered.

To many people, mummies seem scary and mysterious—but not to the Chinchorro of South America. These people, who lived more than 7,000 years ago, believed that the bodies of family members who had died would bring good luck to the living. As a result, the Chinchorro turned their dead into mummies and brought them home.

A mummy found near El Morro

Although the Chinchorro were a simple people who hunted and fished to survive, they created a very **complex** process for making their mummies. First they sliced into the corpse and removed muscles and major **organs**, such as the heart and the brain. Then the mummy-makers filled the body with hot coals and ashes to dry it out. Next they stuffed wool, feathers, and other materials into empty spaces. Finally, they placed a painted clay mask over the face. The idea was to suggest that the dead person was merely sleeping. After the mummy was finished, its relatives repaired and repainted it over and over through the years to keep it looking new.

No one knows for sure why the mummies were finally buried near El Morro. One possibility is that people buried them after more family members died and took the older mummies' places among the living.

Chinchorro mummies

The Chinchorro had no metal tools. They used sharpened rocks, shells, and bird beaks to cut into the bodies they turned into mummies.

Curse of the Boy King?

King Tut's Tomb, Luxor, Egypt

The Egyptians believed that their kings, known as pharaohs, were gods who had come down to Earth. After these rulers died, their spirits would continue to live among the gods. The Egyptians also thought that to fully enjoy this afterlife, the pharaohs needed their bodies. So a pharaoh's corpse was turned into a mummy and buried with food, beautiful artwork, and priceless treasures that the pharaoh would take along to the afterlife. Anyone who dared disturb the tomb or remove its riches would be put to death.

In 1922, an English **archaeologist** named Howard Carter explored the tomb of Tutankhamun (*too*-tahn-KAH-muhn), a pharaoh who ruled ancient Egypt more than 3,000 years ago. King Tut is sometimes called the boy king because he came to power when he was about nine years old and died around the age of 18 in 1322 B.C.

The valley where Tut's tomb was found

Like all pharaohs, King Tut was buried with great riches. Also like the others, he was turned into a mummy by highly skilled experts called **embalmers**. The Egyptian mummy-makers began their process by removing most major organs. Then they laid the body in salt to dry it out. Finally, the embalmers wrapped the mummy in strips of cloth and placed it in a magnificent set of nested **coffins**.

After Howard Carter entered King Tut's tomb and found both the boy king's treasures and his mummy, newspapers started printing **legends** about a "mummy's curse." According to these stories, a dead pharaoh would cause great harm to anyone who entered his tomb. When a man who had worked closely with Carter died, some people said the curse was to blame. Scientists, of course, say there is no mummy's curse. Yet that hasn't stopped books and movies from keeping the legend of the pharaoh's revenge alive to this day.

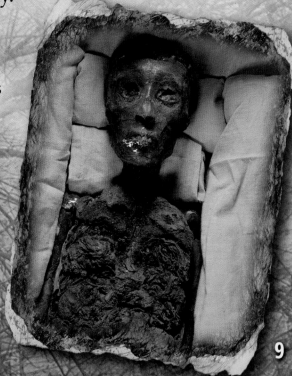

King Tut's mummy

Some newspaper stories claimed that the curse was recorded on a stone tablet in Tut's tomb. The words on the tablet were said to be "Death shall come on swift wings to him that touches the tomb of Pharaoh."

Mummies Underneath a Monastery

The Capuchin Catacombs, Palermo, Sicily

Visitors to the Capuchin **monastery** in Palermo, Sicily, are greeted by an eerie sight. Entering underground tunnels called catacombs, they face rows of mummies—some lying down, others held up by hooks. Many wear their best clothes. That's not surprising, since when the inhabitants of the tomb were still alive, they chose to be turned into mummies after death and displayed for all to see.

Inside the catacombs

The Capuchins are **Roman Catholic monks**. At first, they buried dead monks in a cemetery at their monastery, which was built during the 1500s. Later, when they needed more space to hold the dead bodies, the monks built the catacombs. As the monks went to move the bodies, they noticed that the corpses had been turned into mummies, thanks in part to the dry air in the cemetery.

Soon Roman Catholics in the area learned about the mummies. Some wanted to show their faith by being buried in the catacombs with the mummified monks after they died. The Capuchins learned how to **preserve** the corpses using both the dry air and a mixture of chemicals. Relatives of the dead people often came to visit the mummies and sometimes even brought them new clothes.

Today, thousands of mummies fill four long hallways in the Capuchin mummy lair. Some of the dead were priests and other important people in the local area. Others were everyday people, including children.

Mummies posed to look like they are praying

In 1920, a Palermo **pharmacist** embalmed one of the last bodies that was placed in the catacombs. It took 90 years before the notes he left listing the chemicals he used were found—notes which revealed his secret embalming **formula**.

The Outlaw Mummy

Laff-in-the-Dark Fun House, Long Beach, California

A lair is usually a dark, spooky place, but the mummy of Elmer McCurdy was often displayed in plain sight. McCurdy's mummy spent decades traveling the United States as part of carnivals and other shows before reaching its final resting place in an Oklahoma cemetery.

Elmer McCurdy was a crook who robbed banks and trains during the early 1900s. After taking part in a train robbery in 1911, he was killed by an Oklahoma **posse**. They took his corpse to a nearby funeral home, where it was embalmed. McCurdy's body was not buried, however, because Joseph Johnson, the owner of the funeral home, refused to give it up until someone paid him for his work.

Elmer McCurdy while he was still alive

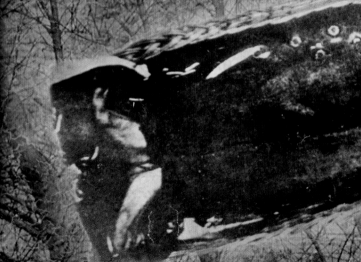

Johnson waited a long time. Five years passed, and no one came to claim the corpse. During that time, Johnson took the mummy—which had not rotted because of all the chemicals he had used in the embalming process—and propped it up in his funeral home. Then he charged people a nickel to see "The **Bandit** Who Wouldn't Give Up."

In 1916, a man who said he was McCurdy's brother showed up to claim the body. He actually ran a carnival, however, and put the mummy on display as part of his show. Over the next 60 years, McCurdy was featured in various carnivals before finally ending up in an amusement park in Long Beach, California. In 1976, a worker there thought he was a dummy—until an arm came off, revealing human bone. The mummy of Elmer McCurdy was finally taken out of show business.

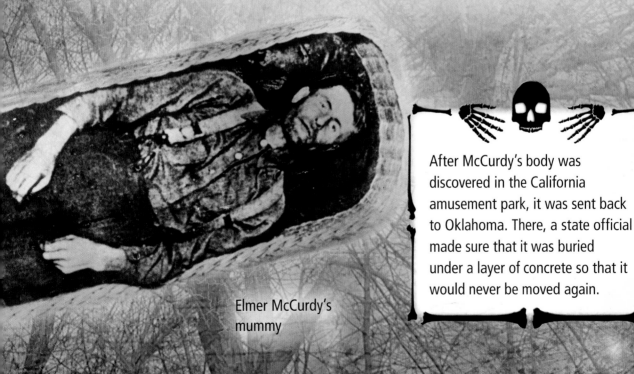

Elmer McCurdy's mummy

After McCurdy's body was discovered in the California amusement park, it was sent back to Oklahoma. There, a state official made sure that it was buried under a layer of concrete so that it would never be moved again.

The Preserved Leader

Lenin's Tomb, Moscow, Russia

Some called him a monster who ordered the murder of thousands of people. Others saw him as a hero who helped make their country strong. He was Vladimir Lenin (1870–1924), the man who led the **Russian Revolution** of 1917, which created the **Soviet Union**. The Soviet Union no longer exists, but Lenin's body remains on display in Moscow, Russia—the country's capital.

Visitors to Lenin's tomb enter a building shaped like a pyramid.

ЛЕНИН

Over the decades, millions of people have filed past Lenin's lifeless body, which lies in a building called a **mausoleum**. After Lenin died, Soviet leaders didn't want people to forget him and his efforts to build **communism**—a political system that was supposed to spread wealth in an equal way. Preserving Lenin's body was one way to honor him.

To prepare Lenin's body for public display, doctors performed some of the same steps ancient mummy-makers did. They removed organs, such as his brain, along with blood and other fluids. Later, experts used a variety of chemicals to keep the body from rotting. About every 18 months, Lenin is removed from his tomb. His body is placed in a special bath that keeps his skin soft. In between the baths, doctors use bleach to wipe away any **mold** that forms on the body.

Vladimir Lenin

Nowadays, fewer people visit Lenin's tomb than before. Russia is no longer a communist country, and some Russians think Lenin's body should be buried. They want to forget all the violence that took place during his lifetime—including the deaths of those who opposed communism.

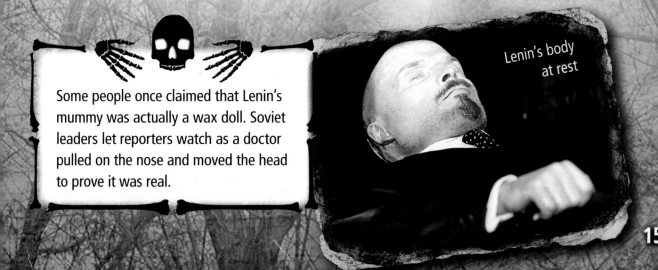

Some people once claimed that Lenin's mummy was actually a wax doll. Soviet leaders let reporters watch as a doctor pulled on the nose and moved the head to prove it was real.

Lenin's body at rest

The Ice Mummy

Ötztal Alps, between Italy and Austria

For two German hikers, a pleasant day in the Ötztal (UHRTS-tol) Alps ended with a strange discovery. Taking a shortcut through the mountains, they saw a large brown object stuck in some ice. Getting closer, they realized the "object" was a dead body. Officials needed several days to free the mummified corpse, which soon earned the name Ötzi (UHRT-see) the Iceman— and turned out to have been on the mountain for a very, very long time.

Ötzi in his frozen lair

Since his discovery in 1991, Ötzi has become one of the most famous of all mummies. Scientists who have examined his remains have figured out that he lived about 5,000 years ago. It was **climate**, not human effort, that preserved his body for all those years. Shortly after he died more than 10,500 feet (3,200 m) high in the Alps, snow and ice covered his body. They kept Ötzi from rotting.

Experts aren't sure who Ötzi was. Items found near the mummy include a copper ax and some arrows. These could mean he was a hunter. Yet some experts think Ötzi might have been a shepherd. In either case, the items preserved in the ice with the mummy offer clues about how people in this region lived long ago.

Another mystery surrounds Ötzi: Why did he die? Scientists know *how* he died. They found an arrowhead in his shoulder and think he bled to death from his wound. But who fired the arrow? Was Ötzi a criminal someone chased and shot? Did he fight with members of his own tribe? The Iceman took those answers with him to his frozen resting place.

Several people connected to Ötzi, including one of the hikers who found the body, died soon after the frozen mummy was discovered. It didn't take long for people to wonder if removing the Iceman's body from its frozen lair had set a deadly curse in motion.

A model showing what Ötzi might have looked like when he was alive

The Mummy from the Bog

Tollund, Denmark

Across northern Europe, damp areas called **peat bogs** have held the remains of people who died several thousand years ago. The bogs are perfect mummies' lairs. Although rotting plants formed them, these swampy places helped stop the corpses from rotting.

The most famous bog mummy of all is Denmark's Tollund Man, who was named for the village near where he was found. In 1950, some local men were digging for peat, which poor people sometimes burn as heating fuel. Cutting into the peat bog, they found the mummy, which is thought to be about 2,400 years old.

The bog where Tollund Man was found

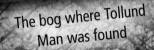

Peat moss

Peat bogs have several conditions that help create natural mummies. Their water is high in acid, which can kill **microbes** that eat dead flesh. The bogs also lack oxygen, something else the microbes need to survive. In addition, a **moss** called sphagnum (SFAG-nuhm) is found in many bogs. It contains a substance that, like acid, kills certain microbes.

Tollund Man is thought by experts to have the best-preserved head of any ancient mummy. Also preserved is the rope around his neck that was used to hang him. The people who placed the dead body in the bog never knew that the peat would create a mummy that would shock people thousands of years later.

Experts think the ancient people of northern Europe sometimes hanged people as **sacrifices** to the gods they worshipped. Tollund Man and other bog mummies were most likely such sacrifices.

Tollund Man

The Dead of Pompeii

Pompeii, Italy

Usually a body must have preserved skin and perhaps even eyes or other soft tissue to be called a mummy. Yet the victims of a long-ago disaster left behind shockingly realistic models of their bodies, even though their flesh completely rotted away. The mummy-like figures even look just as they did at the moment of their deaths. How is this possible?

In ancient times, wealthy Romans built homes in the Italian city of Pompeii to enjoy its pleasant climate. In 79 A.D., however, a nearby volcano called Vesuvius (vuh-SOO-vee-uhs) erupted, shooting out hot ash, poisonous gases, and lava—and causing widespread death and destruction.

A mummy in Pompeii

For hundreds of years, Pompeii lay silent and buried. Then, in 1748, it was finally rediscovered. Digging through the ruins, people studying the city found hard casts of human bodies. These stony outer coverings were formed when layers of rock and ash covered people who couldn't escape the eruption and then cooled over their dead bodies. Inside the casts, some bones still remained, though the skin and organs had rotted away.

In the 1800s, a scientist chipped away at some of the casts and poured **plaster** inside. When this material hardened, it created a kind of mummy that showed what the Romans had looked like when they died—sometimes including a look of horror on their faces. More mummy casts have been made since then. They have been displayed around the world, reminding people of nature's deadly power.

Some of the plaster "mummies"

The eruption of Vesuvius lasted more than 24 hours. The flow of lava rushed down the volcano at speeds of around 100 miles per hour (161 kph).

Mummies of Mexico

Guanajuato, Mexico

The mummies uncovered in Guanajuato (gwah-nah-HWAH-toh), Mexico, have been called "accidental mummies," since no one planned or took steps to preserve them. Instead, these bodies became mummies due to natural conditions while being stored in a crypt. Today, more than 100 are on display in their hometown. Their new lair is called Museo de las Momias— Spanish for "Museum of Mummies."

Inside Guanajuato's mummy museum

Families living in Guanajuato, Mexico, once had to pay a fee to bury their dead relatives. Some were allowed to pay over time, but if the payments stopped, the dead were dug out of the local cemetery. Their corpses were then kept in the crypt next door. In 1865, gravediggers working at the crypt were shocked to open one tomb and find a mummy inside.

The dry air of Guanajuato and the tight seal of the crypt had helped preserve that corpse and others there. Most of the dead were poor working people. It is likely that many were miners or their relatives, since Guanajuato was the site of both silver and gold mines.

Legends swirl around some of the Guanajuato mummies. One female mummy is said to be a woman who was buried alive. The mummy's arms are over her face, not by her sides as with most corpses in the region. Perhaps the woman had been struggling to escape her untimely burial.

Some of the Guanajuato mummies

Another legend in Guanajuato said one mummy was the corpse of a man who had been hanged. Modern science proved that tale wrong, since the body did not have the usual physical damage done by hanging.

The Self-Made Mummy

Gue, India

About 500 years ago, a **Buddhist** monk named Sangha Tenzin did something very unusual. He began a process that would help turn him into a mummy after his death. Why would anyone want to end up this way?

Sangha Tenzin's mummy can be seen inside this building in Gue, India.

According to legend, the remote village in India where Sangha Tenzin lived, called Gue, was infested with scorpions. To help get rid of them, Tenzin began **fasting** and **meditating**. It was said that when he finally died from hunger, a rainbow appeared and the scorpions vanished. In addition, Tenzin left behind a body that looked like a statue in the act of prayer. Sangha Tenzin believed that leaving behind a body that would become a mummy was a sign of his faith.

By starving himself to death, Tenzin had already begun to turn himself into a mummy. Not eating causes the body to lose muscle and use up fat. Having as little as possible of each helps preserve the body later. Once Tenzin was dead, fellow monks put his body in a room where it would dry out even more, completing the mummification process.

The mummy Sangha Tenzin left behind

Tenzin's body was found in 1975, after an earthquake shook him from his lair. He was sitting up, as he would have been when he was alive and meditating. The monk seemed to be carrying out his religious duties even after his death.

Sangha Tenzin's village is located high in the Himalaya Mountains. The cold, dry air there helped preserve him.

Digging for Dog Mummies

Saqqâra Desert, Egypt

Underneath the windswept sands of Egypt's Saqqâra desert are catacombs more than 2,500 years old. Inside the tunnels, scientists recently began studying one of the most amazing lairs ever. It was filled with millions of mummies. These were not the preserved bodies of humans who lived long ago, however. Instead, they were the preserved bodies of dogs.

The Saqqâra desert

Becoming a mummy is not just for humans. In nature, animals have been turned into mummies by the same cold, dry climates that can mummify people. Beyond that, ancient Egyptians made mummies of a wide range of animals. Among them were cats, dogs, cows, birds, and crocodiles. All these animals played an important role in Egyptian religion.

The Egyptians worshipped many gods, including Anubis, a god of the dead. Anubis was thought to have the head of a jackal, a wild relative of the dog. People hoped to win the god's favor by bringing it dog mummies. Some of the mummies were of dogs that had lived in a temple that honored Anubis. Others were of dogs that were raised so that their remains could be offered to the god. In all, the catacombs in the Egyptian desert were filled with eight million dog mummies—a dead gift to a god of death.

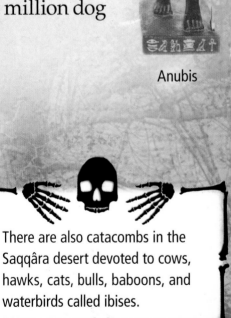

Anubis

A dog mummy from ancient Egypt

There are also catacombs in the Saqqâra desert devoted to cows, hawks, cats, bulls, baboons, and waterbirds called ibises.

Mummy Lairs

Tollund, Denmark

A peat bog became a mummy's lair.

Long Beach, California

An amusement park is the final stop in the career of Elmer McCurdy's mummy.

Ötztal Alps, between Italy and Austria

An icy lair held a mummy for more than 5,000 years.

NORTH
AMERICA

Guanajuato, Mexico

A crypt became a home to more than 100 mummies that were made "by accident."

Pompeii, Italy

Ash from a volcano preserved people at the moment they died.

Pacific Ocean

SOUTH
AMERICA

El Morro, Chile

The world's oldest mummies were found here.

Atlantic Ocean

Around the World

Arctic Ocean

EUROPE

ASIA

AFRICA

Indian Ocean

AUSTRALIA

Southern Ocean

ANTARCTICA

Moscow, Russia
The mummy of a dead leader brings back memories of a bloody past.

Gue, India
A holy man became a mummy to save his village.

Palermo, Sicily
Thousands of mummies line the walls of this lair.

Luxor, Egypt
Did the discovery of a pharaoh's lair unleash a mummy's curse?

Saqqâra Desert, Egypt
Millions of dog mummies fill this lair.

Glossary

archaeologist (*ar*-kee-OL-uh-jist) a scientist who learns about ancient times by studying things he or she digs up

bandit (BAND-it) robber

bogs (BOGS) areas of soft, wet ground

Buddhist (BOO-dist) having to do with a religion founded in India more than 2,500 years ago

climate (KLYE-mit) the typical weather in a place

coffins (KAWF-inz) containers in which dead people are placed for burying

communism (KOM-yoo-*niz*-uhm) a system of government that puts all power in the hands of one political party and limits the amount of property people own

complex (kom-PLEKS) hard to do

corpse (KORPSS) a dead body

curses (KURS-iz) things that bring or cause evil or misfortune; spells

embalmers (em-BAHM-urz) people who preserve dead bodies

fasting (FAST-ing) not eating

formula (FORM-yoo-lah) a list of ingredients used to make something

legends (LEJ-uhndz) stories handed down from the past that may be based on fact but are not always completely true

mausoleum (*mawh*-zuh-LEE-uhm) a large tomb, often made of stone, that sits aboveground

meditating (MEH-dih-*tay*-ting) sitting silently while focusing on a single thought

microbes (MYE-krohbs) tiny, simple living things that can eat flesh

mold (MOHLD) a living thing that is neither a plant nor an animal and grows on damp surfaces

monastery (MON-uh-*stair*-ee) a place where people who have devoted their lives to their faith work and live

moss (MAWSS) a fuzzy green plant that sometimes covers rocks or tree bark

organs (OR-guhnz) parts of the body, such as the lungs, that do a particular job

peat (PEET) soil from a wet area that is made up of decayed plants

pharmacist (FARM-uh-sist) a person whose job it is to make medicines and drugs

plaster (PLASS-tur) a mixture of water and tiny bits of rock that hardens as it dries

posse (POSS-ee) a group of people called by a sheriff in order to help enforce laws

preserve (pri-ZURV) to make last

Roman Catholic monks (ROH-muhn KATH-uh-lik MUHNGKS) men who have devoted their lives to the Catholic church and are part of a religious community

Russian Revolution (RUSH-in *rev*-uh-LOO-shuhn) the overthrow of the Russian government in 1917 that led to the creation of the communist country the Soviet Union

sacrifices (SAK-ruh-*fyess*-iz) people or animals killed as part of a ceremony or as an offering to a god

Soviet Union (SOH-vee-uht YOON-yuhn) a former country that was centered around Russia and had a communist government

tombs (TOOMZ) rooms, buildings, or graves where dead bodies are kept

Bibliography

Aufderheide, Arthur C. *The Scientific Study of Mummies.* Cambridge: Cambridge University Press (2003).

El Mahdy, Christine. *Mummies, Myth and Magic in Ancient Egypt.* New York: Thames & Hudson (2002).

Quigley, Christine. *Modern Mummies: The Preservation of the Human Body in the Twentieth Century.* Jefferson, NC: McFarland & Company (2006).

Wieczorek, Alfried, and Wilfried Rosendahl, eds. *Mummies of the World.* New York: Prestel Publishing (2010).

Read More

Lunis, Natalie. *Tut's Deadly Tomb (HorrorScapes).* New York: Bearport Publishing (2011).

Malam, John. *100 Things You Should Know About Mummies.* Broomall, PA: Mason Crest Publishers (2011).

Sloan, Christopher. *Mummies: Dried, Tanned, Sealed, Drained, Frozen, Embalmed, Stuffed, Wrapped, and Smoked . . . and We're Dead Serious.* Washington, D.C.: National Geographic Kids (2010).

Learn More Online

To learn more about mummy lairs, visit
www.bearportpublishing.com/ScaryPlaces

Index

About the Author

Michael Burgan has written more than 250 books for young readers, including books about vampires, Bigfoot, Frankenstein, and aliens. He lives in the high, dry desert of New Mexico but has never come across a natural mummy.